Firsts in Flight

by Elena Martin

STECK-VAUGHN
Harcourt Supplemental Publishers

www.steck-vaughn.com

Contents

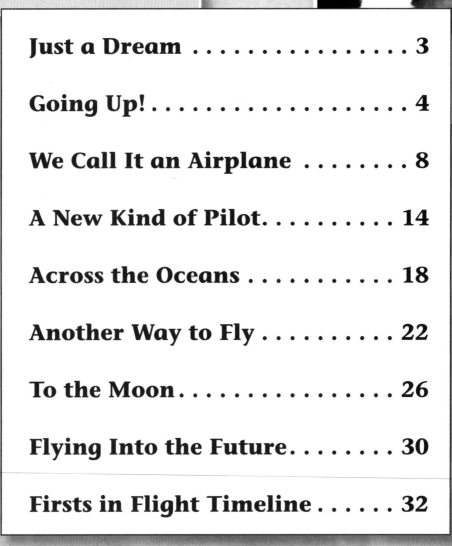

Just a Dream

Long, long ago, people dreamed about what it would be like to fly. Some people drew plans of flying machines. A few people put wings on their arms and tried to fly like birds. But these people were never able to make their ideas work.

Going Up!

Smoke rising from a fire sparked an idea.

About 200 years ago, someone finally did find a way to fly. One day, a man named Joseph Montgolfier saw smoke rise up from a fire. That gave him an idea. Joseph built a wooden frame covered with cloth. Then he built a fire under it. Hot air made the frame rise. It was flying!

Hot air balloons were the first flying machines that worked.

Joseph and his brother started working together to make a hot air flying machine. They tried different plans and shapes. They found that a round shape worked best. At last, they built a big, beautiful balloon. It was taller than a house! But who would ride in it?

Many people came to watch the first hot air balloon flight.

Before any people could ride in the balloon, the brothers had to make sure it was safe. They put a rooster, a sheep, and a duck in the balloon basket. The animals flew for a short distance. Soon after, two brave men flew in the hot air balloon.

People today have hot air balloon races.

Today, many people like to fly in balloons. Hot air balloons still look much like the one built by the Montgolfier brothers. But now balloons fly higher, faster, and farther. They are often made of brightly colored material and can be seen from very far away.

The Wright brothers stand in front of their bike shop.

Many years later, two other brothers dreamed of flying. Their names were Wilbur and Orville Wright. Wilbur and Orville had a bike shop in Ohio. When the brothers were young, they loved to build kites and fly them.

A man flies one of the first gliders.

One day, Wilbur and Orville read about a man who had made a glider. The glider looked like a big kite. A person was able to ride in the glider. The Wright brothers wanted to make something that flew even better.

Men tried to fly an early flying machine that did not work.

For years, Wilbur and Orville learned about flying. They wanted to learn everything they could about things that could fly. They watched birds. They read about kites and gliders. They even read about other flying machines that did not work.

The Wright brothers flew a glider they built.

Wilbur and Orville did experiments, too. They built kites to see which shapes would fly the best. They built gliders and flew them at windy beaches. But kites and gliders need wind to fly. The brothers wanted to make a machine that could fly without the wind.

The brothers began to build another machine. The machine had an engine to give it power. The brothers added parts so that a person could fly the machine. Wilbur and Orville Wright called their machine a "Flyer." And in 1903, it flew!

The first airplane flight lasted only 12 seconds.

The Wright brothers kept finding ways to make their airplane better. They built new planes that could make turns and dive in the air. Their later planes could fly even farther. They could stay up in the air for over half an hour.

A New Kind of Pilot

Flying early airplanes was a dangerous job.

When airplane flying was new, the people who built the planes flew them. Soon, other people wanted to fly planes, too. But flying the early airplanes was a hard job. Pilots sat out in the open, even in the cold and rain. When the planes broke down, the pilots had to know how to fix them.

Bessie Coleman was an African American pilot.

Bessie Coleman was an African American woman who wanted to fly planes. She knew that being a pilot would be a difficult job. But she was determined to learn how. Like many early pilots, she loved the adventure and excitement of flying.

Bessie Coleman got her flying license in France.

Flying lessons cost a lot of money. So Bessie saved her money. She left her home in the United States and went to France. Bessie learned to fly there. She was the first African American woman to become a pilot.

People loved to watch Bessie Coleman's stunts at air shows.

When Bessie returned to the United States, she flew in air shows. Bessie could make her plane dive and loop. People called her "Queen Bess, the world's greatest woman flier." Because of her, many other African Americans and women became pilots, too.

Across the Oceans

This early plane was called a biplane.

By 1928, airplanes were getting bigger. They could fly for many miles. Pilots were flying airplanes across the United States without stopping. Planes were crossing the ocean. Pilots flying over the ocean had to fly for 20 hours or more. There was often heavy fog that made it hard to see.

Amelia Earhart was known all over the world.

Amelia Earhart was a famous pilot at this time. She was the first woman to ever fly across the Atlantic Ocean. Cities held parades for her. She gave speeches and wrote a book about her trip. She showed the world that women pilots could fly long distances, too.

Amelia Earhart flew great distances alone.

The first time she crossed the Atlantic, Amelia flew with two other pilots. She wanted to make this journey all by herself. She tried it four years later, and did it! She became the first woman to fly across the ocean alone. Amelia also made the trip faster than anyone had before.

Fans greeted Earhart after her flight across the Atlantic Ocean.

Amelia had become an even bigger star. She began giving talks about flying. She wanted more people to become pilots. She wanted everyone to know that flying in airplanes was safe. Amelia also wanted women to know that they could do anything.

Another Way to Fly

People watch an early helicopter in flight.

Planes were getting better. But people were still trying to think of new ways to fly. Some people were trying to build a machine that could fly and hold still in the air. They were trying to build a helicopter.

The autogyro looked like a cross between a helicopter and an airplane.

The first helicopters were hard to fly. They bumped from side to side. They tipped over easily. An early kind of helicopter called the autogyro used the body of an airplane with spinning blades on top. It worked better than the first helicopters, but it was still hard to control.

Sikorsky's helicopter was the first to fly well.

Then in 1939, an inventor named Igor Sikorsky made a helicopter that really worked. It could fly straight. It did not tip over. Igor's helicopter had two sets of spinning blades. It had a big set on top and a little set on the back. Most helicopters today are still made in this way.

A skycrane drops 2,000 gallons of water on a forest fire.

Today, helicopters can fly backwards. They can stay in one place while up in the air. They can land almost anywhere. A special kind of helicopter called a skycrane is strong enough to lift thousands of gallons of water. Firefighters use skycranes to help put out forest fires.

To the Moon

Astronauts have flown all the way to the moon.

When people first dreamed of flying to the moon, they thought that they could sail there by boat. That idea seems very silly now! But people have gone to the moon. They have even walked on it. So how did people get there?

Rockets were the first machines to fly in space.

Many people worked together to build machines that could fly in space. These machines were called rockets. The first rockets zoomed up into space, then circled around the Earth. They were only able to make one trip into space.

Neil Armstrong, Michael Collins, and Buzz Aldrin were the first astronauts to fly to the moon.

In 1969, three astronauts from the United States took a special trip. They were going to fly to the moon. It took the astronauts three days to fly there. Neil Armstrong was the first person to walk on the moon. He said, "That's one small step for man, one giant leap for mankind."

Buzz Aldrin was one of the first astronauts to walk on the moon.

The astronauts collected moon rocks to bring back to Earth for people to study. They also put up a United States flag. The astronauts returned to Earth a few days later. But the flag and their footsteps are still on the moon.

Flying Into the Future

Space shuttles can make many trips into space.

Today astronauts travel on space shuttles. The shuttles take astronauts to the International Space Station. This is a building in space about 240 miles above Earth. Astronauts live there for months at a time. They do experiments to learn more about space.

Scientists work to design flying machines of the future.

Scientists hope that the International Space Station will be completely built by the year 2006. Scientists are using what astronauts have learned on the space station to design machines that could fly to other planets. What kinds of future flying machines can you imagine?

Firsts in Flight Timeline

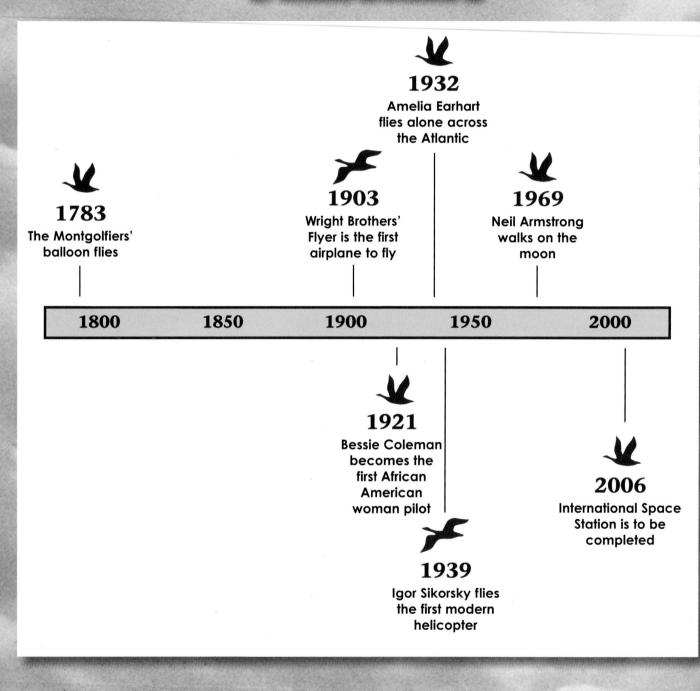

1932
Amelia Earhart flies alone across the Atlantic

1783
The Montgolfiers' balloon flies

1903
Wright Brothers' Flyer is the first airplane to fly

1969
Neil Armstrong walks on the moon

| 1800 | 1850 | 1900 | 1950 | 2000 |

1921
Bessie Coleman becomes the first African American woman pilot

1939
Igor Sikorsky flies the first modern helicopter

2006
International Space Station is to be completed